Writing Stories

Funny Stories

Anita Ganeri

Heinemann
LIBRARY

Chicago, Illinois

© 2013 Heinemann Library
an imprint of Capstone Global Library, LLC
Chicago, Illinois

Edited by Dan Nunn, Rebecca Rissman,
and Sian Smith
Designed by Joanna Hinton-Malivoire
Original illustrations © Capstone Global
Library 2013
Picture research by Ruth Blair
Production by Sophia Argyris
Originated by Capstone Global Library Ltd
Printed and bound in China by South China Printing
Company Ltd

ISBN: 978 1 4329 7534 0 (Hardback)
ISBN: 978 1 4329 7541 8 (Paperback)

17 16 15 14 13
10 9 8 7 6 5 4 3 2 1

Cataloging-in-Publication Data is available at the
Library of Congress website.
Ganeri, Anita, 1961-
  Funny stories / Anita Ganeri.
    pages cm.—(Writing Stories)
  Includes bibliographical references and index.
  ISBN 978-1-4329-7534-0 (hb)—ISBN 978-1-4329-
7541-8 (pb) 1. Humorous stories—Authorship. 2.
Creative writing. I. Title.

PN3377.5.H86F86 2013
808.3—dc23   2012043117

Acknowledgments
We would like to thank the following for permission
to reproduce photographs: Alamy p.5 (© Jeff
Morgan 07); Shutterstock, background images
and design features, pp.4 (© Sergey Dolgikh), 6
(© Yayayoyo),7 (© Zurijeta), 8 (© paulaphoto), 9
(© Losevsky Photo and Video), 12 (© Sandra van
der Steen), 14 (© Kristina Postnikova), 16 (© Eric
Isselée), 18 (© MikLav), 18 (© MisterElements), 22
(© szefei), 24 (© balounm), 24 (© Sandra van der
Steen), 24 (© Kodda), 24 (© Pavel V Mukhin).

Cover photographs reproduced with permission of
Shutterstock (© Sandra van der Steen, © Kodda, ©
bonchan, © Kalenik Hanna, © Pavel V Mukhin).

Every effort has been made to contact copyright
holders of material reproduced in this book. Any
omissions will be rectified in subsequent printings if
notice is given to the publisher.

Some words are shown in bold, **like this**. You can find out what
they mean by looking in the glossary.

Contents

Follow this symbol to read a funny story.

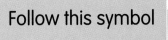

What Is a Story?

A story is a piece of **fiction** writing. It tells the reader about made-up people, places, and events. Do you like writing stories? Before you start, you need to choose a **setting**, some **characters**, and a **plot**.

There are many different types of stories.
You can write mystery stories, animal
stories, fairy tales, scary stories, adventure
stories, and so on. This book is about
writing funny stories.

Writing a Funny Story

You can write a funny story about anything. Let your imagination run wild! Your story can take place anywhere and at any time. You can have fun making up **characters** that are people, animals, or even aliens!

Lots of people like hearing funny stories because they make them laugh.

Your funny story needs to be able to entertain your readers. Try using a mixture of ordinary and funny or unexpected **settings**, events, and characters. This will help make the funny parts seem even funnier.

Ideas, Ideas, Ideas

You can get ideas for stories from books, the Internet, TV, or your imagination. You might see or hear something funny while you are in school, in the park, or out shopping. This can spark an idea for a story.

Have you ever had a really good idea
for a story, then forgotten it? Keep a
notebook and pencil handy for jotting
down ideas. Then you can look at them
when you are ready to start writing.

What's the Plot?

Like any story, a funny story needs a good **plot**. The plot is what happens in your story. It needs a beginning, a middle, and an end. You can use a **story mountain** to help you plan out your plot.

Middle
The main action happens. There may be a problem for one of your characters.

Beginning
Set the scene and introduce your main **characters**.

Ending
The problem is solved and the story ends.

Your story starts at one side of the mountain, goes up to the top, then goes down the other side.

Sometimes it can be tricky to put the events in the right order. A **timeline** can help you. Here is a timeline for the funny story in this book.

Girl goes on a birthday trip to the zoo.

⬇

The zoo has a new star attraction—a T. Rex.

⬇

The T. Rex escapes.

⬇

A dinosaur expert is called in to find it.

⬇

The girl helps him look for clues.

⬇

They find footprints and bite marks.

⬇

They track down the T. Rex at the beach.

⬇

They bring the T. Rex back to the zoo.

In the Beginning

Your story needs a strong beginning that grabs your readers' attention right away. It should make them want to keep reading. It is also where you introduce your main **characters**.

Can you turn any of these ideas into story starters?

- A dinosaur arrives at the zoo.
- An alien lands in your yard.
- A pet cat starts talking.

A Funny Story

Lucy woke up early. It was her birthday, and Mom and Dad were taking her to the zoo. Lucy couldn't wait. The zoo had a new star animal—a totally amazing T. Rex! Lucy had never seen a real-life dinosaur before.

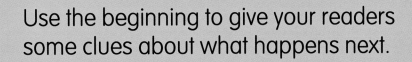

Use the beginning to give your readers some clues about what happens next.

Story Setting

The **setting** means the time and place where your story happens. Think about what your setting looks, sounds, and even smells like. This will help you picture it better. The setting for this story is a zoo, like the one below.

Lucy loved the zoo. Some areas were like a rain forest. Some were like a desert. The animals had big, roomy enclosures to roam around in as well as keepers to take care of them. Lucy loved listening to all the animal noises. She even liked the smell!

Try to bring your setting to life for your readers.

In the Middle

The middle of your story is where the main action happens. It is also where something usually goes wrong for your **characters**. Here are some of the things that could happen in your funny story.

The T. Rex escapes from its enclosure.

The T. Rex eats its keeper.

A lion eats the T. Rex.

The T. Rex loses its teddy bear.

Can you think of any other problems?

But as Lucy reached the
T. Rex enclosure, she heard people
screaming and shouting.

"He's gone!" yelled a woman.
"The T. Rex has escaped!"

Lucy looked around. It was
true. In the fence around the
enclosure, there was an enormous,
T. Rex-shaped hole.

Character Building

You need to make your **characters** interesting, so that your reader cares about what happens to them. Think about what they look like, how they behave, and their likes and dislikes. Jot down the details in fact files, like the ones below.

Character fact file
Character: T. Rex [dinosaur]
Age: Not known
Looks like: Big body; short arms; sharp teeth
Personality: Fierce; hungry
Likes: Eating other dinosaurs and ice cream
Dislikes: Being stuck in a zoo

Character fact file
Character: Dr. D. Hunter [dinosaur expert]
Age: About 40
Looks like: Crumpled clothes; wears glasses
Personality: Smart; kind; nutty
Likes: Dinosaurs
Dislikes: Things that are not dinosaurs

The T. Rex and Dr. Hunter are two of the main characters in our story.

Suddenly, a crumpled-looking figure pushed through the crowd. He was wearing glasses and carrying a large backpack. It was the famous dinosaur expert, Dr. D. Hunter. The keeper showed him a photo of the T. Rex. He was smiling and sticking out his tongue.

"Keep your photo," said Dr. Hunter. "I know what this beast looks like."

Can you also write a fact file for Lucy?

Making a Mind Map

It is easy to get stuck when you are trying to figure out what happens next in your story. Try making a **mind map**, like the one below, to help you move the action along. Write down one key idea. Then add any words or ideas that are connected to it.

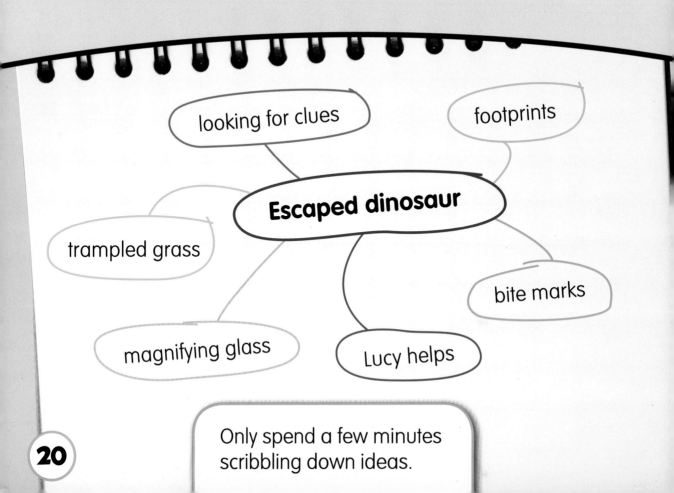

looking for clues

footprints

Escaped dinosaur

trampled grass

bite marks

magnifying glass

Lucy helps

Only spend a few minutes scribbling down ideas.

Dr. Hunter looked at Lucy. Lucy looked back.

"I'm going to need an assistant," he said. "To help me look for clues. Do you want to help?"

"Ooh, yes, please," said Lucy.

"Okay, you'll need this," said Dr. Hunter, handing Lucy a magnifying glass from his backpack. "You look for footprints. I'll check for bite marks."

 Use the ideas from your mind map to keep the action going.

Using Speech

Using **dialogue** in your story brings your **characters** to life. Dialogue means the words that people say. It can help show what your characters are thinking and feeling. It can also make the action feel more exciting.

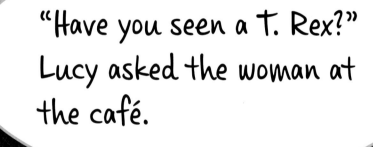

"Have you seen a T. Rex?" Lucy asked the woman at the café.

Put **quotation marks** around the spoken words.

"Have you seen a T. Rex?" Lucy asked the woman at the café.

"He bought a cup of coffee and then went that way," the woman said. She pointed at some gigantic footprints in the trampled grass.

"Have you seen a T. Rex?" Dr. Hunter asked a bus driver.

"Oh, I've seen him!" the driver said, pointing at some enormous teeth marks in the side of his bus.

 Dialogue helps bring your readers into the action.

Exciting Writing

To make your writing more exciting, choose your words carefully. Try out different ways of writing your sentences to make them more interesting.

1 Lucy and Dr. Hunter reached the beach. Lucy was surprised.

2 Eventually, their search led them to the beach. Lucy couldn't believe her eyes!

Which piece of writing sounds more interesting?

Eventually, their search led them to the beach. Lucy couldn't believe her eyes! The T. Rex was sitting happily on the sand, licking an ice cream cone.

"I knew it," said Dr. Hunter. "He just wanted a day out. But I bet he's ready for lunch now. Let's turn around and see if he follows us."

Try reading your story out loud to see if it sounds exciting.

25

Happy Ending

The ending of your story is where your **characters** solve their problems. It is also where you tie up any loose ends. The end can be happy or sad, or have a clever or surprising twist. Here are some ideas for endings for the story in this book.

Endings

- The T. Rex dives into the sea and swims away.
- The T. Rex goes to live with Dr. Hunter.
- The T. Rex follows them back to the zoo.

Which ending would you choose?

Lucy and Dr. Hunter stepped forward and Lucy peeked over her shoulder. Sure enough, the T. Rex was close behind. They led the T. Rex home, and he gobbled down an enormous lunch.

"What will happen to him now?" asked Lucy.

"I've spoken to the keeper," said Dr. Hunter. "They're going to take him for lots of days out. Oh, and for lots of ice cream cones!"

Can you write a different ending to the story?

More Top Tips

1 Read through your story when you finish and correct any mistakes. It may take you several tries before you get it right.

2 Reading your story out loud can help you tell if it sounds right. This is especially useful when you are writing **dialogue**.

3 Read funny stories written by other authors. These can help to spark ideas when it comes to writing your own stories.

4 You can make up some funny or serious **characters**. The main thing is to make them believable, so that readers are interested in what happens to them.

5 Retell your story from a different point of view. For example, you could retell the story in this book in the voice of the T. Rex.

6 Try writing a **sequel** to your story. What happens next to the characters? Does the T. Rex have any more adventures?

Glossary

character person in a piece of writing

dialogue words that characters say

fiction piece of writing that is about made-up places, events, and characters

mind map diagram showing everything you can think of about a subject

plot what happens in a story

quotation marks marks that show the words someone has spoken

sequel follow-up to a story

setting time and place in which a story is set

story mountain mountain-shaped diagram that helps you plan out a story

timeline list of events in the order in which they happen

Find Out More

Books

Ganeri, Anita. *Writing Stories*. Chicago: Raintree, 2013.

Stowell, Louie, and Jane Chisholm. *Write Your Own Story Book*. Tulsa, Okla.: EDC, 2011.

Warren, Celia. *How to Write Stories* (How to Write). Laguna Hills, Calif.: QEB, 2007.

Web sites

Facthound offers a safe, fun way to find Internet sites related to this book. All of the sites on Facthound have been researched by our staff.

Here's all you do:

Visit **www.facthound.com**

Type in this code: 9781432975340.

Index